Matti and Massi Missions

Matti and Massi Missions
ROME

To Luke + Emily, I hope you love to read as much as Mattie + Massi love to explore! ♡ Zeina

Zeina Hamad

Illustrated by Ana Karina Quintero Villafraz

SPRING CEDARS

Copyright © 2021 by Zeina Hamad

All rights reserved

First edition, 2021

Illustrations and book cover by Ana Karina Quintero Villafraz
Book design by Spring Cedars

ISBN 978-1-950484-07-2 (paperback)
ISBN 978-1-950484-08-9 (hardback)
ISBN 978-1-950484-09-6 (ebook)

Published by Spring Cedars LLC
Denver, Colorado
info@springcedars.com
springcedars.com

To Massimo, for all the ways you remind me of Italy.

Captain Smiley

Mrs. Smiley

Massi

Matti

Mission Coach Francesca

Chef Paola

Mission Tools

"This is your captain speaking. Please buckle up and enjoy the flight to Rome, Italy!"

Matti and Massi fastened their seatbelts and gazed out the window as their airplane took off into the blue skies. They had just learned about Rome in class with Mrs. Smiley and couldn't wait to join Captain Smiley's next flight to see the city in person. The Smiley family traveled a lot, but this was no ordinary family trip. This time, Matti and Massi had a Mission to complete.

When the plane landed in Rome's Fiumicino airport, passengers began to disembark.

"Hey dad!" Massi waved toward the cockpit.

"That was a great landing, so smooth," said Matti, fist-bumping his pilot dad.

"Okay boys, I need to prepare the airplane for our flight home," Captain Smiley said. "That should give you enough time to complete the Mission and return before takeoff. Your Mission Coach is waiting for you at arrivals. See you soon!"

Matti spotted their names on a greeting sign.

"**Ciao**! **Sono** Francesca!"

"**Ciao**, Francesca. I'm Matti, and this is Massi."

"Great to meet you. Here is your Mission Bag. We don't have time to waste."

The boys opened their Mission Bag, and the digital timer automatically started the countdown from 6 hours. Matti and Massi stared at the Mission Checklist with great confusion.

"Francesca, what do we have to do?" Matti asked.

"Your Mission is to complete all the tasks and return to your dad's flight before the digital timer goes off. Don't forget you must collect a piece of evidence from each task to place into your Mission Bag. If you fail to finish the Mission Checklist correctly and in time, the flight will depart without you, and you will be left behind in Rome."

Matti and Massi read the Checklist out loud.

Inside the Mission Bag, they found a Polaroid camera, a digital timer, two train tickets, a marker, five euros, two paintbrushes, and a map.

"**Andiamo**! Let's go! We have a train to catch," Francesca shouted, reaching for the train tickets in the Mission Bag.

Matti, Massi, and their Mission Coach Francesca ran across the station and squeezed through the train doors just as they were closing. They used their time wisely on the ride, with Francesca explaining the map of Rome and what the Mission Checklist entailed.

"**La prossima fermata é Colosseo**," the train conductor announced.

"The Colosseum! That's our stop!" Francesca said.

Massi peeked at the digital timer: 5 hours and 30 minutes left.

Matti grabbed the Mission Bag. "You heard her, **andiamo**!"

"Woah!" the brothers exclaimed in unison as they exited the dark underground train station and burst into the bright outdoors.

Incredibile! Francesca smiled with pride. "This is the Roman Colosseum. It was built during the ancient Roman times as an amphitheater for gladiator competitions and public shows."

"It's so big!" Matti exclaimed.

"Can we go inside?" Massi pleaded, hands clapping and eyelids batting.

They looked at the digital timer. Down to 5 hours and 15 minutes.

"**Rapidamente**!" Francesca agreed.

As Matti and Massi entered the circular Colosseum, their Mission Coach explained more about the amphitheater's history and architecture. "This was built in the year 70 CE. Notice the big arches and different levels of seating."

"What is that?" Matti pointed to the maze-like stage at the center. "How could people walk on that floor with so many gaps in it?"

"That is actually below the original floor. It's where the gladiators and animals waited before coming out for their shows," answered Francesca. "Now, we need to move on. **Andiamo**!"

The Colosseum was nearly out of view when Massi suddenly stopped. "Wait! We didn't pose as gladiators or collect our evidence!"

They hurried back and spotted a ticket salesman dressed in a gladiator costume with a shield and sword. Matti asked if they could borrow his props.

"One euro," the man replied, opening his hand.

The euros in the Mission Bag proved useful.

Massi took his combat role very seriously, swinging the sword and grimacing, while Francesca used the Polaroid camera to snap a picture of the dramatic scene. They were having so much fun that they nearly lost track of time, until Matti pointed to the digital timer.

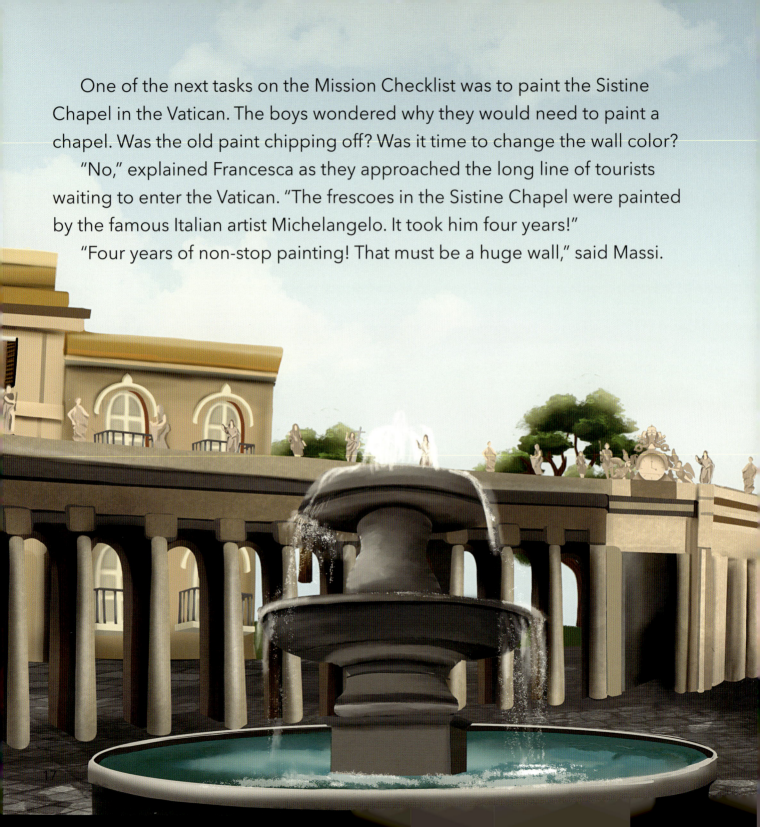

One of the next tasks on the Mission Checklist was to paint the Sistine Chapel in the Vatican. The boys wondered why they would need to paint a chapel. Was the old paint chipping off? Was it time to change the wall color?

"No," explained Francesca as they approached the long line of tourists waiting to enter the Vatican. "The frescoes in the Sistine Chapel were painted by the famous Italian artist Michelangelo. It took him four years!"

"Four years of non-stop painting! That must be a huge wall," said Massi.

The line was moving slowly, and the digital timer was ticking.

"We have to make use of our time," Matti said. "Let's double task."

The trio looked at their Mission Checklist and scouted the area.

"**Gelato**! Massi pointed.

"Good work, Massi. Wait here." Matti grabbed three euros from the Mission Bag and ran to the gelato stand. The vendor handed him three big cones wrapped in white napkins. "**Grazie**!" Matti thanked the vendor and hurried back to the line.

"Quick! Eat before it melts. We can't let any of it drip," Matti reminded the group.

They licked, slurped, and gulped at full speed. "BRAIN FREEZE!" they screamed, squinting their eyes and rubbing their foreheads.

It was almost their turn to enter the Sistine Chapel. Matti and Massi put their clean gelato napkins in the Mission Bag for evidence, next to the pictures from their gladiator photoshoot. The digits on the timer read 3 hours and 55 minutes.

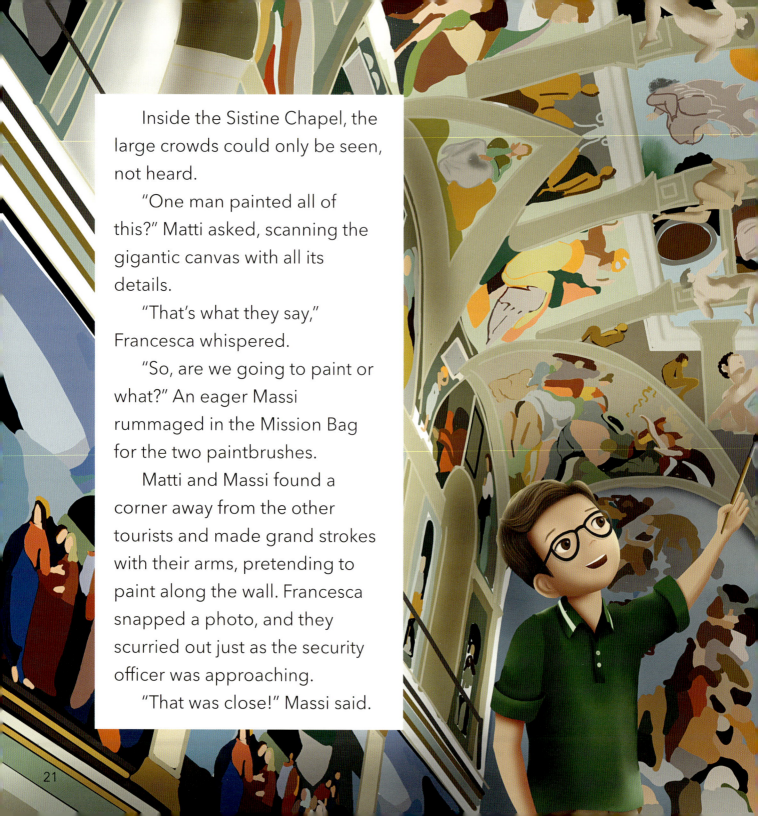

Inside the Sistine Chapel, the large crowds could only be seen, not heard.

"One man painted all of this?" Matti asked, scanning the gigantic canvas with all its details.

"That's what they say," Francesca whispered.

"So, are we going to paint or what?" An eager Massi rummaged in the Mission Bag for the two paintbrushes.

Matti and Massi found a corner away from the other tourists and made grand strokes with their arms, pretending to paint along the wall. Francesca snapped a photo, and they scurried out just as the security officer was approaching.

"That was close!" Massi said.

After checking the map, Francesca led the brothers to a hilltop. "You know what those are?" she asked.

Both Matti and Massi shook their heads no.

"The Spanish Steps! **Andiamo**!"

The trio began their descent, counting each step in Italian. "**Uno**, **due**, **tre**, **quattro**, **cinque**, **sei**…**centotrentotto**!"

"One hundred thirty-eight!" echoed Matti. "How can we prove we counted them?"

"We're down to one euro and three hours, so something free and quick," Massi advised.

Matti opened the Mission Bag. "The marker!" He wrote a big 1 on the back of Massi's hand, a big 3 on the other, and passed the marker to Francesca. "Write an 8 on my hand, please," he said.
   The Mission Coach did as instructed then took Matti's other hand and drew a smiley face. "Just for giggles," she added.
   The brothers held up their hands with a cheesy smile, and Francesca clicked away for yet another photograph.

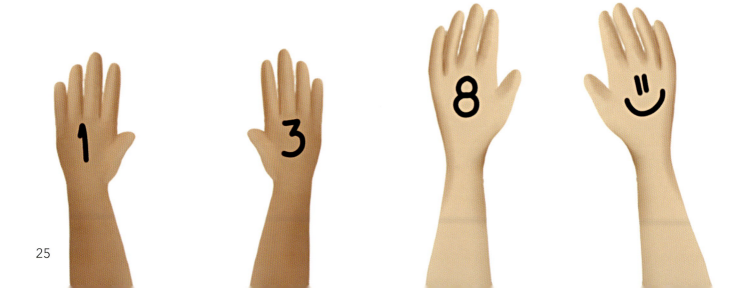

    They reviewed the Mission Checklist and realized they still had two more tasks before their flight would take off: make a wish at the Trevi Fountain and learn the difference between Roman and Neapolitan pizzas.

    "We need your expertise, Mission Coach. Can you tell us about the different pizzas?" Matti asked.

    "I only know how to eat pizza. We need to find an expert," answered Francesca.

The trio headed down the cobblestone streets, following their map to the Trevi Fountain.

"You only have one euro left in your Mission Bag," Francesca noted. "Who's going to toss it into the fountain and make the wish?"

"I am," Matti and Massi answered in sync.

Francesca laughed. "Maybe you can hold hands and toss it together."

"No way!" the brothers replied.

They walked in silence, pondering over the coin-toss dilemma.

But Matti was a great problem solver. "We need to earn some money. We can't come all the way to Rome and not each get to make a Trevi wish," he said.

"Okay, but how?" asked the Mission Coach.

Massi was unusually quiet.

Francesca nudged him. "Do you have any talents?"

"Singing!" he exclaimed. Massi was always brave and outgoing, which sometimes embarrassed his older brother.

"Oh no, please don't give him ideas," Matti pleaded.

Massi started to skip down the road, singing a little tune. Some passersby looked with skeptical eyes. Others gave him an encouraging thumbs up. Just as the trio turned a corner and entered the plaza with the Trevi Fountain, Massi upped his performance. He placed his hat by his feet, then danced and sang his heart out. Tourists stopped to watch, charmed by the entertainer.

Matti facepalmed and retreated into the crowd that had formed around his little brother, while Francesca prompted the tourists to feed Massi's hat. Within minutes, there were enough coins in the hat for the trio to make four wishes each!

"That was **fantastico**!" Francesca applauded. "But it cost us precious time. Trevi wish, then pizza. **Andiamo**!"

As they stood in front of the massive marble fountain, the brothers and their Mission Coach closed their eyes, made their wishes, counted to three, and released their coins.

"We didn't take a photo!" Matti said.

"**Ancora**!" suggested Massi, "We have extra euros. Let's do it selfie-style."

And with that, the trio tossed their second coins and snapped the shot.

There was only one task left. Could they find a pizza expert and make it back to the airport in ninety minutes?

"Pizza expert, where are you?" Massi hollered.

"What are you doing, **sciocco**?" Francesca elbowed him.

"Seriously Massi? That's not how you find one," added Matti.

Ciao!

An elderly woman popped out. "**Sono un'esperta di pizza**!"

The startled trio turned around. Did Massi's cry for help really work? Maybe he wasn't so foolish after all.

Massi grinned and gave his brother and Mission Coach a wink. "We need to know the difference between Roman and Neopolitan pizzas," he said.

The woman was wearing an apron and name tag that read Paola. "**Facile**!" she replied, pointing to the sign above her head. "**Benvenuti nel mio ristorante**."

They stepped into what looked more like a pizza museum than a restaurant. The walls were covered in black and white photos of grandmas kneading dough and sweaty men standing in front of large brick ovens.

"I know everything about pizza. It's been a family business for five generations. **Sedetevi**!" demanded Paola.

The three guests sat down.

"The main difference between the two pizzas is in the dough," the expert explained. "**Pizza Romana** is thin and crunchy from edge to center, whereas **pizza Napoletana** has a thick, soft crust and a thin, floppy center. Let's taste a **margherita e mozzarella** shall we?"

The offer was tempting, but was pizza really worth missing the flight?

Matti opened the Mission Bag. The digits on the timer read 55 minutes. "Francesca, how long is the ride back to the airport?" he asked.

"Thirty minutes, if you're lucky," she replied.

"You can't leave Rome without tasting my famous homemade pizza!" Paola interrupted. "It will be ready in ten minutes. Then, I can drive you to the airport by Vespa, it's quicker!"

Matti and Massi looked at their Mission Coach with pleading puppy eyes.

"**Bene**, but we eat one slice, and the rest we pack to go," said Francesca.

Matti, Massi, and Francesca were seated on the Vespa with helmets on so they wouldn't lose any precious time, and Paola soon brought out a slice of steaming hot, thin-crusted Roman pizza. The trio gobbled it up, ignoring the fact that they had burned the tips of their tongues.

"That was worth everything!" Massi cheered.

Everyone laughed, and Paola handed them a cardboard box. "Pizza to go. Proof for your Mission Bag and a slice for the Captain."

"**Grazie**! **Andiamo**," shouted Matti.

They sped off toward Fuimicino airport.

Matti and Massi thanked Francesca for the incredible adventure and rushed to check-in for their flight, with merely minutes to make it on board before take-off.

"Wait! We're here!" the brothers hollered, just as the plane door was closing.

While running at full speed, Matti and Massi caught a glimpse of their dad through the cockpit window. He waved and smiled while shaking his head.

"**Andiamo**!"

They were safe…this time.

Andiamo — Let's go

Buon Viaggio — Have a good trip

1 Uno 2 Due 3 Tre
4 Quattro 5 Cinque 6 Sei
7 Sette 8 Otto 9 Nove 10 Dieci

Bene — Good

Vespa

Ancora — Again

Facile — Easy

Ristorante — Restaurant

Ciao — Hello/Goodbye

Fantastico — Fantastic

Gelato

Grazie — Thank you

Sedetevi — Sit down

Rapidamente — Quickly

Mozzarella

Margherita

Sciocco — Silly

La prossima fermata — The next stop

About the Author

Zeina Hamad graduated from the University of Virginia and earned her Master of Education from Marymount University. She is an elementary school teacher and has taught in the United States, Spain, and Dubai. You will often find Zeina on her yoga mat, reading a book, or traveling the world with her husband and two kids.

@mattimassimissions

About the Illustrator

Ana was born in Venezuela, lived in Spain, and is currently based in France. Growing up, drawing was always Ana's favorite pastime. She has a special talent in bringing stories to life through her detailed and colorful illustrations. When she is not drawing, Ana can be found dancing salsa, eating chocolate, or sipping coffee.

@ana.kqv

Visit Zeina and Ana at **https://springcedars.com/matti-massi-missions/**